The Do's and Don'ts of Grief

To Wallace
Hoffman,
God will turn your
mourning into joy.

[signature]

THE
DO'S AND DON'TS
OF GRIEF

HOW TO HANDLE
GRIEF AFTER A LOSS

SALLY J. KNIPE

XULON PRESS

Xulon Press
2301 Lucien Way #415
Maitland, FL 32751
407.339.4217
www.xulonpress.com

Unless otherwise indicated, Scripture quotations taken from the Holy Bible, New International Version (NIV). Copyright © 1973, 1978, 1984, 2011 by Biblica, Inc.™. Used by permission. All rights reserved.

Printed in the United States of America.

ISBN-13: 978-1-54564-347-1

'Grief' can be the result of any loss.

Ask yourself: "How do I get through
this journey?"

"Is there anything I can do to make it easier
to walk through?"

"How can I help someone else live through
this time?"

DEDICATION

TO MY PRECIOUS LATE HUSBAND, JIM

with whom I have spent over a half century loving.
And to my dear family and friends who
have supported me so well through this
journey.
And to my Lord Jesus Christ,
Who has been my comforter, defender
and protector. You have been
there for me every step of the way.
For this, I am forever grateful.
And to my dear friend and fellow writer, Norma, who
did a wonderful job editing and encouraging
me with the writing of this book.

"for the Lord will
be your everlasting light,
and your days of sorrow
will end."
– Isaiah 60: 20b

TABLE OF CONTENTS

Dedication vii

Preface xiii

Chapter 1 –   Grief is a Journey 1

Chapter 2 –   Go into 'Survival Mode' 8

Chapter 3 –   Think... Before You Give. . . . 12

Chapter 4 –   Grieve Your Own Way. 19

Chapter 5 –   What Can I Do For
              the Family? 26

Chapter 6 –   Where is YOUR Faith? 32

Chapter 7 –   The 'Whys' and the
              'What Ifs. 39

Chapter 8 –   Name Your Day! 45

Chapter 9 –   'The Widow's Mite'. 52

Chapter 10 – Anxiety and Fear 57

Chapter 11 – The Five Stages of Grief 66

Chapter 12 – "Relapses" 82

Chapter 13 – Your Legacy - "What are 'YOU' leaving behind?". 89

Chapter 14 –What's Next?. 101

The Journey of Grief 109

Epilogue 113

Endnotes 115

Other Resources 119

Other Books by Sally J. Knipe. 121

About the Author 123

PREFACE

You are walking through life and you feel like all is 'normal.' 'Normal' will be different for each of us. Normal is everyday living where there are no real tragedies facing you. The day may even feel mundane to you and you just get up each morning and go about whatever it is you do.

THEN, without warning, you are in the midst of a crisis. A loved one is ill, your spouse says they're leaving the marriage, your mammogram is abnormal or your husband dies after 53 years of marriage. The man I've known since I was 15....the man I've loved for 56 years....is suddenly gone.... Shocking, to say the least. Devastation and sadness like you've never felt creeps in and you are in the middle of this scary 'journey of grief.' You have never traveled this road to this extent and the unknown has brought you to your knees.

You ask yourself, "How will I ever get on the other side of this deep pain?" "How will I ever smile again....or have purpose in my life?" "Will life ever be 'normal' again?" So, what do you do?

I don't pretend to have all the answers; nor do I have a degree in psychology, but I pray this simple reading can give you some fundamental practices as you walk this journey of grief. We go through it step by step not knowing what to expect around the corner. It's one of the most heart wrenching times of your life, but, you *will* get to the other side. You've heard the term 'new normal' and you will eventually have a 'new normal' but it will be forever different because that special something or someone is gone. There will be light at the end of the tunnel and you will survive the journey, but some days you doubt it. *Good* will even come out of your pain and sorrow but, in the beginning, you cannot see that happening and you definitely never want to say that to a newly grieving person. None of those easy comments will ever help a person walk this journey. Beware of sayings like:

1. 'He (she) is in a better place.'

2. 'At least your loved one isn't suffering anymore.'
3. 'Look at all the years you had together.'
4. 'God must have wanted him (her) home.'
5. 'All things work together.'

God will use even the worst tragedy for your good and His glory; but never, ever say that to a person in the beginning stages of their grief. These comments sound trite and often cause hurt rather than comfort. If you don't know what to say at least tell them, "I am so sorry to hear about your loss. It must be so hard for you right now." Telling someone who's hurting that you are sorry, at least lets them know you care.

Not saying anything about the person's loss is hurtful as well. They are hurting deeply and, when you don't even mention it, they could interpret that as you not caring. It's okay if they cry when you say something comforting to them. They are in the depths of pain and usually want to talk about the person or situation. You don't have to ask for details, but if the person wants to talk about their pain, let them. It is therapeutic for the grieving person if you are kind and listen. It was helpful for me to talk about Jim's death and what led up to it. Be the 'safe' friend the hurting person can come to and share what they are going through.

I pray the simple truths in this book will give you guidance and help you on your journey of grief. Bless you and may God's peace be with you, especially now. His peace does not depend on our circumstances. His peace is always there as we walk and endure our circumstance. Just call on Him.

CHAPTER 1

GRIEF IS A JOURNEY

*"Grief walks with
me wherever I go. I know that
You, God, are on the other side
of me holding my hand and
sometimes holding me up."
– Sally J. Knipe*

September 15, 2017 Entry from my
personal journal:

"I feel like I'm on the verge of slipping off a mountain and I am trying, with everything in me, to keep from stumbling. Thinking about my future without Jim is daunting, and scary and just plain sad. Right now life seems all too much. It's all overwhelming and the future feels unsafe without my 'other half.' Yet, I know without a shadow of a doubt, that You are there with me every minute, of every day."

You are on one of the hardest trips you have ever had to travel. The road is one of twists and turns and you never know what is around the corner. You feel exhausted from the trek yet you don't seem to have a destination. You fear going off the edge and you huddle where it seems safe. Whether it's the death of a loved one, a major health diagnosis, a divorce, a wayward child strung out on drugs or alcohol, grief comes in many forms and we suddenly are thrown into this pain and sorrow we have never felt before. We thought maybe we could relate to that friend that lost her husband, but we really can't; we can only console.

My grief started when my sweet husband of 53 years died after complications of falling from a tree. I told him to let a professional trim that tree, but he was a man that could do most anything and he forgot he was almost 75. He didn't look his age and he certainly didn't think he needed to do anything different than he had done all the years of our marriage. If something needed to be done he did it.

August 14, 2017 Journal Entry:

> "I ask, how do you let someone go that you have loved for 56 years? You don't! Someone once taught me that as people age we lose our health, our mind, maybe our eyesight, our independence. The only two things we keep are our memories and our faith. No one can take them away from us. This is equally true when a loved one dies. I still and will always see the fruit of Jim's faith and have our precious memories. They are like 'precious gems' to me."

I met Jim at the age of sixteen on a blind date. It was love at first sight. Yes, we were young, but we knew what love felt like and after three years we were married. I guess you could say, we grew up together. With God's help, we made it to 53 years. I can say I loved Jim even more over the years and we had a good and healthy marriage and for that I am ever grateful. But when you are an *item* that many years, you feel like someone ripped half of your soul from you.

Six weeks after falling off a ladder and breaking his pelvic bone, Jim's heart began to deteriorate and he died six weeks later. We all were in shock! One day we would walk into the intensive care room and think, "He's going to make it." The next day we would walk in and say, "I don't think he's going to make it." I remember one day my sweet daughter-in-law spent the day with me at the hospital and things did not look good. She had brought her office work with her and I gazed over at her and asked, "Deb, what do you think? Is Dad going to make it?" She got up from the window seat and came right over and hugged me and sobbed these words, "Mom, I think Dad's dying." It was not a surprise to me to hear these words but it brought a sad reality to the situation. Jim died a little over a week later, and so I began the journey of grief. It is never a path we choose to walk, but when a tragedy hits you square in the face, you have no choice.

Sometimes we may grieve a situation when a loved one is slowly deteriorating in their health. We may grieve through the time of their illness and not feel the extreme impact of grief when their death is fairly predictable. We will all grieve in different ways and we will walk through those famous 5 steps of grief, which I will cover in a later chapter. But GRIEF does have many common facets. Let me mention a few:

1. *Grief will always catch you off guard, no matter how well you have prepared for it.*

2. *Grief is personal to each of us.*

3. *Grief hurts and takes time to walk through; there is no easy way, except maybe to go into denial.*

4. *Grief will take its toll on you physically, mentally, emotionally and spiritually. Expect it!*

5. *Grief is NOT the time to isolate yourself from others. You need family, friends, and the body of Christ and possibly a professional*

of some type. You need 'safe friends' to talk to openly and honestly.

6. *Grief can make you feel like you are going crazy. You will not be able to think clearly, sleep well, concentrate, remember things, or see tomorrow. You feel like your world, as you knew it, has stopped. Grief is so unpredictable.*

7. *Grief will end one day, but make sure you don't rush through it. You need to go through it completely. They say your grief journey can take anywhere between 2 to 5 years, depending on the situation. Of course, the memory and loss will never go away.*

8. *Grief is very hard work. The journey leaves you exhausted. Let grief have its way. You will heal someday! You will get on the other side of this journey. Someday you will see spring again. Your life will have meaning again. 11. 12.*

9. *There is no right or wrong way to grieve.*

10. *Own your own grief. It is yours and no one else can take it from you.*

"Our time on earth
is a school.
'Grief' is the toughest class
we have to take."
–Unknown

CHAPTER 2

GO INTO 'SURVIVAL MODE'

"And the God of all
grace...will Himself
restore you and make
you strong, firm and
steadfast."[1]

What exactly is 'survival mode'? Years ago,
when our two oldest children were 6 and 4
years old, I suffered a period of deep depression
where I could not even leave the house at times.
It lasted about two years and I learned then how
to go into survival mode. Survival Mode is basi-
cally getting through each hour or minute of
each day doing whatever you have to do to just
'get through'. You know the Bible says, "When
all else fails, just stand." Sometimes standing
is all you can do. The survival mode sounds
simple, but it really becomes your friend.

I remember after Jim died, Sundays were always very hard for me. Sundays we usually spent all day together...going to church, making lunch at home together, taking a nap and watching football. How could I get through Sundays without Jim? I'd wake up and feel like sobbing and panicked about the day. For the first many Sundays I went into survival mode. I would call someone in the morning for prayer. One day I had called my oldest daughter. My son-in-law answered the phone and he talked and prayed with me. It was so special. I would either invite myself to one of my children's homes or make plans with a friend. Little by little Sundays got better and they weren't so devastating.

Do whatever you need to do to survive and get through the day. People will usually understand and talk with you, pray with you, have you over or plan an outing with you. If you are having a bad day you may have to cancel a commitment and get out of the house and do something more enjoyable. Don't be afraid to be honest with those around you. Make things happen. I found that people totally understood and were there ready to help me through an especially rough day.

My first Thanksgiving alone, the kids planned for our family to go to a cabin in the White Mountains. It seemed to be a good idea...and it was, but Thanksgiving Day was so hard for me. My son-in-law knew I wasn't doing well when I took my third walk around the block. I just couldn't get on top of the anxiety I felt and even though I was surrounded by my loving kids and grandkids, the loss was intense. I enjoyed the day as much as I was able, and I just got through it by taking walks, naps and praying. At one point my dear granddaughter got in bed with me and just held me. It is those little things that help you get through the hardest of times. Be mindful of that when others are going through the depths of grief.

I managed to get through Thanksgiving and even enjoyed the time we hiked and picked out Christmas trees, as well as the fun times of playing games. Our family always has a lot of fun together and we all felt comfortable reminiscing about Jim. What would Dad be doing right now? It all helps and you do get through it.

Be sensitive if someone around you is grieving. Reach out to them in tangible ways and help them survive those rough days. I was never one to ignore the 'elephant in the room.' That person is in the depths of grief and ignoring it does no good at all. There may be a few people that really prefer not to talk about their pain, so respect them concerning this.

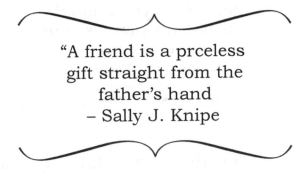

"A friend is a prceless
gift straight from the
father's hand
– Sally J. Knipe

CHAPTER 3

THINK... BEFORE YOU GIVE

"There are times to give out
and times to take in. Let
others serve you and take
care of you when it's your
time to receive."
– Sally J. Knipe

Your loved one dies, and what happens? The food, the flowers, the fruit baskets begin to roll in almost at record speed. I was the recipient of so many gifts. I received more flowers than I knew what to do with and ended up having an allergic reaction. One morning I was sniffing so badly from all the flowers I asked my brother-in-law, who was staying with me, to take them over to my daughter's. That ended up not being such a good idea. They woke up to all the flowers in their kitchen and immediately their house guests began to sniffle and not be able to breathe. My point is to think before you give.

Flowers or a fruit basket are the most common gifts sent to those who are grieving. Before you send a floral arrangement make sure the recipients aren't allergic to them. Think of the convenience at a time when even the smallest of tasks is too much. It actually takes time to pull apart a fruit basket and refrigerate it. I know it sounds silly, but it all can be overwhelming.

Let's think out of the box. How about taking a simple basket of fruit or a book to read later? Or a gift card to a local grocery store. Then, if you are hosting out of town guests, you can get the breakfast and lunch foods you need. How about a tray of lunchmeat and cheeses. Or maybe a restaurant gift card so the grieving family can take their visitors out. Feeding people is the last thing on your mind when you are making tons of phone calls and running here and there to make the arrangements for the funeral or memorial service. How about offering your services to help set up the meal after the funeral or service? Time is a wonderful gift. I had many girlfriends pitch in and take over setting up and cleaning up from the lunch after Jim's memorial service. My daughter-in-law, Debra, made all the reservations for the facility where the service was to be held.

Jim died in the hospital around 9:00 am the morning of August 1. We were able to stay in the hospital room with him another hour as family gathered. Even a few close friends showed up. The hospital brought us coffee and goodies while we were saying our goodbyes. Our daughter offered us her home to hang out after we left the hospital. Her home was fairly central to where our friends and family lived. Within thirty minutes the food, drinks, and desserts starting pouring in. Carloads... mind you! Friends backed up their SUV's and pulled out tray after tray of goodies and bottles of water. We had enough food for lunch and dinner. People came and went all day long and into the evening. It was so nice. These are all practical ways to help and give to the mourning family. And don't forget to bring paper products.

So think beyond flowers and fruit baskets. Think about the best way to show your support and love. I received promises for a lunch date down the road, and visits from those who couldn't make the memorial service.

One of the best gifts I received was my sister-in-law and her husband came to stay with me for two weeks. We kept playing this game of "Should you come now or wait?" Finally, one day I felt the Lord impress on me strongly that *'yes'*, they should come now. The next day they were here from Pennsylvania. What a sacrifice. This is Jim's only sibling and we are very close. They stayed with me and drove me back and forth to the hospital. It was nice to have someone drive me when I was so tired or it was dark out. After Jim's death, they were there to support me in whatever I needed...ordering food, meeting with the pastor who was doing the memorial service, and the man who would coordinate the service at the church where it was to be held. They were there in the evenings to keep me company. It was so comforting having their presence with me every step of the way that first week after Jim's passing.

My two sisters and their husbands did not come to Jim's memorial. I encouraged them not to come because there is so much going on and it would not have been a good visit. They had been so supportive throughout his illness with their many calls and prayers sent our way.

But what they did, was spend a week with me, individually, a couple months after Jim's death. This was a huge gift to me. We cried together, laughed together, played a lot of games, went shopping and out to eat. We were just sisters together. Their two weeks with me were timely and greatly appreciated. That was as much a gift to me as all the other things people gave and did. One sister had already experience the loss of a husband so she understood what I was going through.

So think before you give. I know it's customary to send flowers, but ask yourself, "Would _____ appreciate something else?" "Would some other form of a gift mean more down the road?" Let God impress upon you what would mean the most to the person who lost their loved one.

One of the best gifts while Jim was fighting his battle was the love and prayers and calls I received day and night. You want to keep people in the loop and they really want to know what is going on. This can be exhausting, so you may consider Websites like Caringbridge.com. This is where others can log onto the site and put in the person's name and get updates. This is so helpful for those going through the trial. My computer savvy daughter set the whole thing up for me during one of her visits and it was so helpful. You are just too exhausted and distraught to keep up with everyone, yet you want them to have the latest news and condition of the patient or situation.

Each of us has something to give. When others are hurting and grieving this is the time to give out. Ask what they need. Remember the family members are also grieving and need to be cared for. This is the time to let your gifts and talents shine whether you are an encourager, a server, or a behind the scenes type person. Maybe you are a giver or a person that is 'just there' for whatever needs to be done. Being a good listener can be a great gift as well. You don't need to give a solution or an answer. It is just good to let the hurting person vent.

The rules are the same in the case of an illness or tragedy. Do whatever you need to do to help ease the situation and minister to the hurting people who are dealing with the grief and pain. Maybe their house needs cleaning or being readied for guests. Don't be afraid to step up and ask, "What would help you right now?" Then, make sure you follow through.

A dear friend of mine asked me a few weeks after Jim's death, "What do you need that you're not getting?" That's a wonderful question. Remember, the grieving process goes on for the hurting person long after everyone returns to their normal life.

"Sometimes the best gift is
just your love and caring.
Knowing someone else cares,
is often enough to get you
through another minute,
another day."
– Sally J. Knipe

CHAPTER 4

GRIEVE YOUR OWN WAY

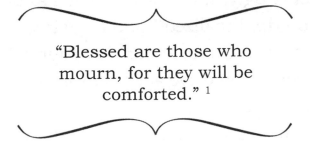

"Blessed are those who
mourn, for they will be
comforted." [1]

Journal Entry, September 9, 2017:

"Last Saturday I hit the lowest of the
low. My children were all out of town
and I was alone most of the day. The
plaque of loneliness surrounded me
and the enemy took full advantage of
my vulnerability. I began to hear lies
floating in my thoughts. "Why live?"
"You don't want to live alone the rest
of your life." "You should do something to yourself so you can be with
Jim." I had to stand against those
thoughts and tell them out loud to

shut up and go away. Depression has settled in like a well fitted jacket and it scared me to recognize the depth I had fallen."

Grief is ugly. It drags you down and tries to beat you up. I realized I had to go into 'survival mode' and that particular day I forced myself to get ready and drive across town to one of my favorite stores.

Everyone grieves differently and individually and we have to allow ourselves and others to grieve their own way.

Shortly after Jim died I felt a distance between my daughter-in-law and myself. I thought I was imagining it because we have always had a close relationship. You can't trust your own emotions when you are grieving. I felt hurt and warned myself that I was just reading too much into this.

I had a garage sale soon after Jim passed away. To others it may have seemed uncaring to go through his clothes and tools and get rid of what the kids didn't want. But I was running high on adrenaline and I couldn't relax if I had to. Another ingredient of grief is you often

cannot relax or sleep either. Dangerous combination! My daughter-in-law has a servant's
heart and she did not come around even to help
set up the garage sale. She did call late on the
day before the sale to see if I needed any help.
As I pondered this I felt like I heard the Lord say,
"Let everyone grieve their own way." Wow...what
a revelation! I found out later that Deb could not
come to the house with her father-in-law not
there because it was too hard. Deb and Jim had
a very close relationship. She loved him dearly
and he loved her like a daughter. I finally understood and told myself not to take this personally.

The Thanksgiving after Jim died, I had mentioned that the family decided to spend the hol-
iday by renting a cabin in the White Mountains.
My youngest son, Eric, did everything in his
power not to go. He did not ask off work which
he would have gotten off. He just did not want
to go, even though he would not come out and
admit that. Eric was our very first foster child.
He was 6 months old when we first took him
into our family. He is now 38 years old. He knew
no other parents but us. Jim took Eric under his
wing and taught him how to do life, everything
from changing the oil in his car to how to be a

patient fisherman. Jim would stop whatever he was doing to take Eric fishing at our local lake. Eric just couldn't face going somewhere different for Thanksgiving without his dad. He preferred going to close friends where things were familiar. We each have to grieve our own way.

My oldest son may not show a lot of outward emotion, but he is a very loving man. He couldn't hold his tears back, as he shared at his Dad's memorial service. Even some friends could not come around because they, too, were grieving the loss of their dear friend. Many men were affected by Jim's death because he had mentored and loved them. Jim touched so many lives.

My youngest daughter, Persis, grieved the loss of her Dad as her *encourager*. Jim was always quick to listen when she would call on the phone and share her newest business idea. Our oldest daughter, Lynn, struggled with some anger as to why God took her Dad. When Lynn called on the phone and Jim answered it, he would always say, "Hello firstborn." Jim loved well so it was hard to realize he was gone from this earth for the rest of our lives. Our oldest granddaughter thought the whole family would fall apart now that her Papa was gone.

Jim invested in people's lives. He certainly left a legacy, which will be covered later.

Personalities come out to their fullest during times of death and severe illness. Our ugly side may show as our emotions are raw. We must give each other the benefit of the doubt and give them permission to grieve *their* way. This is not a time for conflict and family feuds. The enemy would love to cause division at these times of pain, but we must 'tell our self the truth' and not take up offense.

Some friends will stay their distance and others will cover you with love and support. Friends you thought would be there may not be, while other friends will surprise you and be right there by your side. The morning Jim passed away two of my close girlfriends came to the intensive care unit to pray. A nurse saw them in the waiting room and told them that Jim had passed and they could come into the room if they wanted. It was comforting for me to have them there. Not everyone would be comfortable with that, but they were very close friends and just cried with us as we said our final goodbyes. One of them went home and baked delicious cookies and made some food to bring to Lynn's. What a friend!

Some men just sobbed on my shoulder and others were too uncomfortable around me. With time friends came around. They told me they were just too sad to see me.

Let this be your rule of thumb: Don't look at what people don't do. Rejoice in what people do and how they reach out to you.

In the case of a long illness or a divorce, people may just not know what to say. Sitting with you and hugging you or praying may just be enough. Sometimes laughter really helps. It is truly like a medicine. We all react differently to pain and sorrow. Give one another permission to grieve their own way. Give yourself or another person the time they need to grieve. It's a process we cannot hurry.

I ended my journal entry that very devastating day by saying: "As I said before, God never wastes a thing, especially our suffering for He will use it in the future to glorify Himself and to encourage someone else walking through a similar valley."

"In the beginning grief goes with
you wherever you go. It is like an
unwanted companion. You may
forget your circumstances for a
while but grief always returns.
It takes courage to walk this journey
and not want to give up along the
way. Grief is never easy and takes so
much energy to get to the other side.
When you are grieving be easy on
yourself and treat yourself to the
little pleasures of life around you.
At least we have a loving companion
right beside us who knows grief'
only too well."" – Sally J. Knipe

CHAPTER 5

WHAT CAN I DO FOR THE FAMILY?

"There is always something you
can do for the grieving family.
If you don't do something at the
time of the death or tragedy,
do something soon after to
show your love and support.
Doing nothing only hurts those
grieving as it says to them you
don't care, whether that is true
or not." – Sally J. Knipe

Let me remind you that grief comes in many shapes and sizes. It is not just the death of a loved one; it is a major loss of any kind. Whether it involves a career loss, business setback, broken relationship, death of a favorite pet or moving from a dear friend, all of these are losses that need to be grieved. Of course you would reach out differently in each case scenario, but do REACH OUT. Don't give the excuse, "Well, I don't know what to do." Or "Maybe I would be horning in." *Reach out anyways!*

In a previous chapter I discussed what to send a grieving family or individual. But how can I help the family after a few days or weeks have passed. Something as simple as a note, a text, an email, a card (how about a handmade card), or phone call to ask the simple question, "What do you need?" can be comforting for sure. Ask them, "Tell me a practical way I can help." People are not going to contact you when you say, "Let me know if you need anything." You can barely get up and walk through the day and you definitely don't have the mindset or energy to call someone and say, "Oh, by the way, would you do some errands for me?" Let me suggest some very practical ways to help:

1. If out of town guests and family came, offer to clean the linens and the house after the guests leave.

2. Take over a grocery store gift card or offer to pick up some food for a meal or two.

You and a friend can do this together. Put your food in containers that don't need to be returned. Offer to grocery shop for the grieving family or person.

3. Take over a gift card to a restaurant so the family can go have dinner and relax.

4. Pay them a visit or call and just listen. It is very helpful and therapeutic for the grieving person to talk about what happened. They may tell their story over and over again.

5. If the loss is a job termination, money or groceries would be especially valuable to the hurting family.

6. Offer to run some errands. There are always many matters to take care of. It is such a demanding time for the family, so doing the smallest thing can really help. As I mentioned earlier time is a great gift.

7. Help the person go through paperwork. In the case of a death, there are mounds

and mounds of paperwork and forms to be sent in to various businesses and utilities, and financial or banking institutions. It is very overwhelming.

8. If you cannot reach out in the beginning, reach out to the grieving person or family as soon as you can. Some close friends of ours did not contact me for several weeks after Jim's death. This really hurt me and I had an opportunity to talk to the wife at a gathering and share how I felt. The very next day, they called me and we met for lunch and talked over all that had happened and 'why' they hadn't been in touch. This really saved our friendship.

I met a friend in the grocery store several weeks after Jim passed and she said, "What is something I can do?" I told her I missed playing cards since my partner is no longer around. Playing games and cards was one of our favorite past times with friends and family. It was a big part of our social life, but when you don't have a partner you are limited. This friend immediately planned in the next few days, a luncheon and afternoon of cards. She invited female friends I hadn't seen for a long time and it was delightful.

9. Just bless the hurting person however God instructs you. A couple of days before Jim's birthday which is right before Christmas, I got a surprise visit from my youngest daughter, Persis, who lives in California. I was so shocked as well as blessed. She said she wanted to be with me on her Dad's birthday. She stayed three delightful days and was I ever blessed. We talked and talked and watched Hallmark movies from my bed. It was such an unselfish thing for her to do for me. Be creative in your giving. Enter the world of the other person to the best of your ability and ask, "What would bless them and make them smile?"

"Throwing a stone into a river causes many, many ripples. When you see what one stone can do in a river, imagine what one kind deed can do when you reach out to a friend in need. A hug, a note, a call, an invite to dinner can change the whole mood of their day."
– Sally J. Knipe

CHAPTER 6

WHERE IS YOUR FAITH?

> "Release the 'I don't
> know why this happened
> moments' to the Lord.'"
> – Pastor Brandon Cormier

September 11, 2017 Journal Entry:

"Dear Father, thank God I have my faith in You. I don't know how I would have made it otherwise. I don't know how I ever got through these last many weeks since my hubby's death. I look back at the dark and desperate path I have walked and I say, 'How?' 'How did I walk such a path?'

Of course, I know there was no way, no way on this earth, I could have walked through and survived these last days without you beside me, holding my, carrying me at times and JUST BEING THERE. No one can walk through this intense pain and heartache without You.

Your comfort and love have ushered me through the valley of despair. The 'sense of loss' is so deep, but You carried me through. Even though I lost the 'love of my life', Your love has been even greater."

If you are reading this book, you are no doubt grieving some loss or buying the book for someone who is. I do not know if you have a faith or where you are on the spiritual spectrum. But this next chapter is mostly speaking to the Christian, even though I believe, all of us can benefit. So please hear me out. I'm just going to be honest here...I don't know *how* you get through tragedy and heartbreak and death without looking to a Higher Power. Without that strength and comfort, I fear you can only get bitter as we have to blame someone that *this* happened to us. IF I did not have my faith firmly in place I could NOT have walked this walk like I have. From the very beginning of this grief journey I have leaned on God like never before.

He, alone, can bring the peace and comfort you so desperately need at these times.

Maybe you are a Christ follower but you are young in your faith. Grieving will help grow you up. I want to encourage you to stay pliable and not allow the root of bitterness take up residency in your heart. We don't know the 'whys' of things that happen. I am not God and neither are you. A beautiful illustration of this is the picture of a tapestry, a wall-hanging. When you look from the bottom up you only see threads dangling and what looks like a mess. But when you gaze at the top, you see a finished handiwork of beauty. You see the complete work. Our lives are exactly like this. We don't see the completed work though, until we get to heaven. The thing we must assure ourselves is that *we get to heaven!*

My dear readers, when a loved one leaves this earth the only comfort we get is that they are in heaven with God. There is no more pain, sorrow, or tears for them. Our time to leave this earth is unknown and we can't just bank on the fact that we will be ready. We must be ready for the day of our passing, by knowing in a personal way, the salvation that comes from our Lord Jesus Christ. We must receive Him as our Savior and Lord and confess that we need Him because we can't save ourselves. As we grieve our loss, remember how God watched His very own Son, who was without sin, die. He watched Him hang on a cross and die a terrible death. God knows the pain of grief. He has walked that journey and will walk it with us. He has felt the pain of a loved one slipping away and He is there with us. He knows sorrow like no other. He knows loss like no other and He has experienced everything we are going through. Why wouldn't we turn to Him who understands? Why wouldn't we run to Him who has 'been there?'

So, I encourage you to make yourself right with God. Life is so unpredictable and uncertain. If you had told me on our last family camping trip in May that Jim would not be here three months later, I would have told you that you were crazy.

I could have never walked this walk without God's love, provision, wisdom and peace. Sure, I asked many 'whys.' But God promises to not only meet our every need, but to be with us every day throughout our life. Not just when we deserve it, or when we need something, or when we are good, but every minute of every day.

When I was so overtaken with sorrow the first many months, I would make myself start naming those things I was grateful for and it helped my perspective. Gratitude changes everything. I have a coaster on my desk that says, "Begin each day with a grateful heart." This shows us that we still have things to be grateful for even in the midst of our sorrow. If you look at other's circumstances, you can always find someone worse off. And you think to yourself, "How are they getting through that?" And I would answer, "The same way you are."

God's grace is only when we need it and as much as we need. His grace, although we want to question that at times, is always big enough for each day and each area of grief. The WW II concentration camp survivor, Corrie Ten Boon, wrote in one of her books that growing up her father would never give her the train ticket 'til she needed it. He would say, "You don't need the ticket until you get on the train."[1] That is exactly how God's grace works. We won't have what we need until we need it.

I remember the tragedy that hit the Christian singer and songwriter, Curtis Chapman, a few years ago. His teenage son accidently ran over his little sister and killed her. I wondered how they got through that. They survived after much heartache and a lot of good has come out of it. He wrote a book and a new song about it and became a stronger man with a stronger family. They did not let this tragedy break them.

God's grace is more than enough and what He promises He does, for God cannot lie.

We always have a choice 'what' or 'who' we go to in our times of need. It is hard not to go to other things for comfort and we have to be careful we don't. A week after Jim died I went out and bought a new leather sofa and ordered a new coffee table on line. It felt good at the time until the visa bill arrived. Of course, that was a onetime spending spree. I just needed something new. We have to be careful 'what' we run to, that won't damage us in the long run. The only safe Person to run to is God, the Creator of the universe and our Father, who dearly cares and loves us with an ever-lasting love.

It's best to know Him before you need Him.

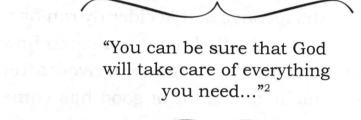

"You can be sure that God
will take care of everything
you need..."[2]

CHAPTER 7

THE 'WHYS' AND THE 'WHAT IFS

"His mercies are new every
morning."[1]
Don't forget to look for
them each day.

Let me warn you right now that the 'whys' and the 'what ifs' will drive you insane. Don't get me wrong, it is very normal to ask 'why' in the beginning. It would probably be abnormal if you didn't. Some of my 'why's' were: "Why didn't the surgeons do the heart procedure sooner?" "Why didn't I make Jim go back to the doctor sooner?" "Why did I let him go up in that tree?" "Why did Jim die so soon?"

My 'what if's' were similar. "Would Jim have lived if he hadn't fallen out of the tree?" Did the fall really begin the decline of his heart?" What caused his organs to deteriorate so fast?" "What would his condition be *if* Jim had lived?"

The questions go on and on and you discuss them with others and you go round and round and can't seem to come up with any good answers. Whatever happened cannot be reversed. As you fill in the blank of your own loss, your questions will be different. There are times in a tragic accident caused by an outside party; or a medical 'mess up,' that you do need answers because more action may be necessary on your part. But in my situation, the 'whys' and 'what ifs' began to have a toll on me and my path to healing. It does take a lot of time to come to the acceptance of what happened, but asking these questions over and over again slow up the healing process. I had to eventually come to the point that Jim was not coming back to this earth. His death was permanent as far as this side of heaven. That's hard and painful.

A big question to God was, "Why weren't all those prayers answered?" Friends and family from coast to coast and even out of the country were praying for Jim and his healing. I know he was healed, but that was not the kind of healing I wanted. One day I was asking God this question and I felt He said to me, "I heard every one of them."

I believe He heard every prayer and caught every tear of mine and those hurting with me, but He didn't answer the way I wanted. I've found that God always does answer. His answers are either 'yes', 'no' or 'not now.' Remember the story of the tapestry. You see, I don't know the whole picture. I don't know what condition Jim would have been in if he had the surgery for his heart. I don't know what quality of life he would have had. But I do know that God wraps His blessings in unexpected wrappings. Many times we miss His blessings because we are looking for a certain outcome, healing, diagnosis, but they don't look like we want. So we miss the gift from God. He wraps it differently and we don't recognize it. We can be nearsighted when it comes to God's blessings and gifts to us.

I remember one evening about 5 months after Jim's death. It was almost dark and I asked God for a gift. I walked outside my house and looked up. There was the most beautiful full moon I have seen in a long time. I knew immediately that the moon was a gift from my

Abba Father. The first months of my grieving, God gave me many, many gifts in the form of other people calling, texting, inviting me over, or a special surprise in the mail. You just have to look up and see the wonders of the Lord!

At one point I realized that by not letting the 'whys' go I was questioning the perfect will of God. I was questioning His sovereignty. God knows what's best; not only for us, but for our loved one and in any situation where we are grieving. I can't always say that for divorces, but God is still in control no matter what. Man will selfishly have his way and mistakes will happen in the medical field, as doctors are human, but God will always be God.

The biggest loss in a broken relationship is the ongoing pain that takes place the rest of your life. As hard as it may sound, even in this, you must get to a place of acceptance and know that God can bring good out of this too. You may know the scripture that says, "ALL things work for the good to those who love Him and have been called according to His purpose."[2] My pastor's wife once said to me concerning this verse, "If it's not good; it's not done." I love that statement. God's principles certainly apply to grief and their ripple effect on you.

I also know that as far as the death of a loved one, that the Bible says that God knows the number of our days,[3] no matter what we think.

Following are some words from my journal that I felt God impressed on me when I asked Him *why.*

August 16, 2017 Journal Entry:

"My dear, I heard every one of your prayers. You know I always do what's best. For Jim and you this was the best. For I know the plans I have for you! I will be with you every step of the way as I already have been. One day it will all make sense when you see me face to face. Carry on, my child, and don't waste your time asking 'why.' Instead, spend your time asking each day, "What now, my Lord, what now?" Lean into Me and I will give you rest. Look to Me and I will give you peace. Follow Me, and I will give you direction. Remain moldable in My hands and your life will have divine purpose again. I am the author and finisher of your faith."

September 15, 2017 Journal Entry:

"I find it hard right now to stay peaceful. My mind races to all those questions like 'Should I do this?' 'Should I do that?' I must remain in Your peace or I will do myself physical and emotional harm from all the upheaval. 'He will take great delight in you; He will quiet you with his love. He will rejoice over you with singing.' [2] "I must rest in You only, especially through this journey of grief."

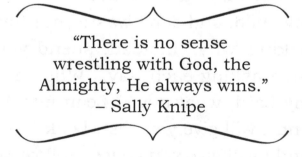

"There is no sense wrestling with God, the Almighty, He always wins."
– Sally Knipe

CHAPTER 8

NAME YOUR DAY!

'Each morning holds the
promise of a brighter
day ahead.'
– (Carlton Cards)

Let me explain what 'name your day' means when it comes to grieving. It may sounds like a game show, but I invented a new tool. It helped me to evaluate what kind of day I was having while I grieved. So I named it. This might sound silly but it really helped me get in touch with my feelings for that day. When I was with friends, or if people texted me and asked how I was, I had an answer. "This is a very sad day." "This is an angry day." "This is a day I feel like I can't go on." "I can't keep my thoughts clear today." Putting a title, so to speak, on my emotions for that day helped me be transparent with how I was really feeling.

When asked how I was doing, I told them honestly. One day I named, "I don't want to be a widow" day. I wasn't doing too good that day!

Shortly after Jim died my oldest daughter, Lynn, asked me what kind of day I was having. I answered, "An angry day." She asked who I was angry at and I answered, "Dad, because he left me with the shed and garage to clean out. He left me with all the outside stuff!" Jim and I pretty much split our chores as far as our home. He said he was CEO of the outside and I was CEO of the inside of the house. But he also remarked one day that sometimes I became CEO of the outside as well. I crossed some boundary lines in other words. So here I was in the middle of an Arizonan summer with the temp over a 100 degrees cleaning out a shed, taking care of our yard and our pool. These were all areas that Jim managed.

Many days I would name, "I don't know how to survive day." Why? Because, in the case of a spouse's death or a divorce, you may be left to understand areas of your lives that you know little or nothing about. Here is some good advice from someone who has walked this path. If you don't know about your finances, or where your personal papers are kept, or how to care for the pool then *find out!* In the case of a spouse's death or illness you will be lost if you don't know the affairs of your home. Find out ahead of time. Where are the titles to the vehicles, in case you have to sell them? Where is the deed to the house, in case you move? Do you have a life insurance policy? Even simple things like how to turn on the heat? That one was simply moving the switch from AC to heat. Thankfully, I always had my son or son-in-law or a friend close by who could come to my rescue. How was I to know all these things? Jim and I discussed most everything and I thought I knew. But when you are grieving, your thoughts are in a fog and you're confused. You must know your finances and who to call in the case of a spouse's death. You need to know where all your important paperwork is kept. I still have not located the deed to our house and I have looked in all the logical places. However you can call the local assessor's office and they will help you out. Please, know what goes on in your home with your finances and medical info. If you have neglected to do this and your spouse has died, then encourage your family and friends to find out all this critical information for themselves. Even something as minor as whether you have towing for your vehicle and who your insurance company is. If you are a widow you need to know these things. It's all very shocking and overwhelming and the more you know ahead of time, the easier it will be when tragedy hits. There are so many couples where only one of them knows the finances and this is not good! Do you pay bills online or do you have automatic *bill pay?* What are your passwords for your online banking and other categories? When do I pay for car insurance, home insurance, etc.? What is the combination to the gun cabinet/safe? These are all things that are helpful to know while your spouse is still alive.

So in order to eliminate too many 'confused days,' I recommend you know as much as you can know about running your home. With today's technology changing so rapidly I feel, as an older person, that it is so hard for us to keep up. Just purchasing a new cell phone and setting it up can be very frustrating if you are not technically savvy.

I end this chapter with a warning. As you name your day, please take inventory of how you are really doing emotionally and physically. If you are prone to depression take extra caution to see if you are slipping into that dark hole. If you aren't sleeping for days on end and can't think and can't cope at all, *please* call your doctor or therapist for an appointment. Because I have dealt with anxiety and depression throughout my life, I could not face going *there again.* You may experience both of these throughout your grief. Watch the levels you sink to. Ask a close family member or friend to keep an eye on you and your condition.

My depression got to a place that it scared me. I called my family doctor and he prescribed something temporarily to help me through this desperate time. I only needed it for a few weeks before I could go off of it. But watch yourself. The combination of no sleep and grief can be deadly. I am not pushing drugs by any means and there are plenty of good natural products that can help you as well. Take inventory of your physical and emotional condition and do something about it or ask someone else to help you. I went to a grief share group before

Christmas that was based on getting through the holidays. There are many groups out there to help. Like me, I didn't want to go, but I forced myself to attend and a dear friend offered to accompany me. It was extremely helpful.

Hopefully, you have a support system that is there for you, to help shoulder your load in tangible and intangible ways. A hug always helped me because I no longer had that physical touch from Jim. The smallest acts of kindness can help the grieving person to get through those sad days.

My children were so in tune to where I was at on any given day and they did so many practical things to help me through that day. My daughter knew that Sundays were a very hard day for me and she asked me over for football and dinner. As I mentioned earlier my youngest daughter, from California, blessed me with a surprise visit. My sons and son-in-law helped me with advertising and selling our truck and travel trailer and listing things on Craigslist. My youngest son would bring fast food home for dinner often. You only get through this journey a day at a time and it's amazing how little things can help you get through another day. Ask yourself, *"What kind of a day am I having today?"*

'Grief will pull you to the bottom
if you let it. It will have its
own way, if you don't fight with
everything in you. At times it
would be easier to give up, but
we still have a life to live and
people who need us. Our job on
earth is not completed. We are
still needed. Don't try to walk
this walk alone.'
– Sally J. Knipe

CHAPTER 9

'THE WIDOW'S MITE'

"Even to your old age...
I WILL sustain you." [1]

Have you thought much about the verses in the Bible concerning the widows and the orphans? I knew the story about the widow's mite in Luke 21:1-4, but other than that, I never concerned myself with the promises God has for providing for the widows and orphans. As I reread these verses after Jim's death, I realized how much my Father cares for these two types of people. I am now a part of one of those groups and I really don't like it.

Whether your loss is a divorce, death, illness or any kind of tragedy, you may be thrown into financial devastation. For me, becoming a widow meant I received less money per month. If you both received Social Security, the amount will be less. You may lose a spouse's pension.

You may have to go back to work or apply for government assistance temporarily, or scale down your living status. You may have to sell your home or one of your cars or move in with one of your children. Don't tell them I suggested that!

I am thankful I am able to stay in my home of twenty-four years. But in order to stay there I have hired a gardener and a pool service. I have never been used to hiring others to fix and repair things around the house, but it was necessary now. Who will do the things Jim always did? My grown sons and son-in-law are wonderful but I don't want them to take on another home to maintain. I will stay as independent as I can for as long as I can.

In the Old Testament there is a reference about the widow: "Do not take advantage of a widow or an orphan. If you do and they cry out to me, I will certainly hear their cry." [2]

In Psalms God also mentions caring for the widow: "(He) is a father to the fatherless, a defender of widows... and He sets the lonely in families." [3]

{Entry from Jim's journal 2017}

'What is pure religion...want to be blessed?'
"Religion that God our Father accepts as pure
and faultless is this: Look after the orphans
and widows in their distress and keep oneself
from being polluted by the world." [4]

But I do have a great provider. He promises to care for me as a widow. And, to tell you the truth, He certainly has taken care of me in so many creative ways.

I happened to be talking to someone who said the state they lived in had a widow's exemption for property taxes. I had never heard of such a thing. I called the local assessor's office and found out how to apply for this discount in my property taxes. My daughter-in-law suggested I go on the Dave Ramsey budget plan. Dave Ramsey founded a financial Christian plan to live successfully with no debt. It can be done! I began to implement that plan.

I have to confess that the Lord provided in ways I would never have imagined. The story of the widow's mite is that while the rich gave a portion, she gave it all. At times of grieving it helps to do what I call, *"thankful therapy."* Make it an exercise to thank God for the things you have and list your blessings each day. As the widow's story in the Bible, I haven't given it all yet.

I remember one day my youngest son Eric and I were out running errands. We were talking about Jim and how we both felt. Eric, in a very nonchalant way, said to me, "You know, Mom, we are kind of like it says in the Bible....you're the widow and I'm the orphan." What perception for Eric to say that. His biological parents *are* dead, but he views us as his real parents who raised him.

Just as God honored the widow's mite, He cared for her needs as well. You may be the one reaching out to the widow who is struggling or just needs a boost. You see from the above Scriptures the importance God puts on caring for the widow and seeing to her needs. It may be something as small as fixing a leaking spigot or taking a baked good to her. You don't know how you are answering someone else's prayer.

Giving to someone else helps you recover. I have found this true throughout my life. When I am down, if I look around and meet the need of someone else, I always feel uplifted. This is how the body of Christ works. When I am down someone lifts me up and when they are down I lift them up. It is like when Moses in the Bible, was told to keep his hands lifted while his people were in battle. When his arms got tired, Aaron and Hur came along to hold his arms up. This is a beautiful example for us to follow. Don't be too proud to receive from others. They are the hands of Christ and just want to bless you and care for you in your time of need.

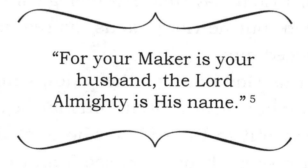

"For your Maker is your husband, the Lord Almighty is His name." [5]

CHAPTER 10

ANXIETY AND FEAR

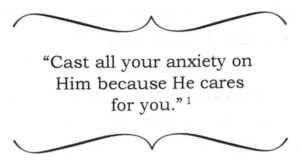

"Cast all your anxiety on
Him because He cares
for you." [1]

September 10, 2017 Journal Entry:

"I believe Paul, from the Bible, dealt
with anxiety and depression. He said
in Philippians 4:6 'Do not be anxious about anything.' He even writes
in Philippians 2:28, 'that I may have
less anxiety.' Paul is so relatable
and so human, yet so godly as well.
I believe he is the David of the New
Testament. As I am suffering, I too
hope I will become more Christ-like
through this time of testing."

October 31, 2017 Journal Entry:

"Yesterday I hit a major wall and my anxiety is off the charts. I thought I was walking this 'grief walk' fairly well, but after three months into it, I feel like I have completely fallen apart. The stark reality of Jim's absence has hit me with such force along with the fact that he will not be coming back. This is my life now and I must accept it and live it. Only you, Father, can pick up the shattered pieces of my life and put me back together."

A few years ago I wrote a children's book about an angel with a broken wing. It was inspired by my grandson, then much younger, breaking a favorite angel of mine that I had displayed on a cabinet in my foyer. *"The Angel with a Broken Wing"* was eventually published and the story line went that only God can mend our 'breaks' and when he does, we are more beautiful than before. Even our grief can add to our beauty and our scars can make us more beautiful than before.

Neither fear nor anxiety is listed as stages of the grief process, but they should be. As someone who has struggled with fear and anxiety throughout my life I can say that a loss of any magnitude can make these emotions surface.

Your life has been turned upside down and nothing is 'normal' as you know it. *If* you thought you were in control, you certainly are no longer. Everything is spinning out of control around you and fear sets in often bringing anxiety with it.

What do I do now? How do I handle things alone? Do I move? Do I stay? Can I make it financially? Where do I turn for help? And I could go on and on. Plug in your own concerns and questions. Your concern may just be, "How am I going to get through this day?" "What lies ahead for me?" "What if I don't get through this illness?" "What about my children?"

The worries can be endless because the future looks so uncertain. However, we must tell ourselves that we were never in control and our future is in God's hands now and will always be. Why? Because He holds the future. He knows the beginning from the end. He knows we will eventually see light again where currently there is nothing but darkness and the unknown. We can trust Him even though we can't see Him. Throughout the Bible it states clearly that He is a God that can be trusted even though we may not understand His ways.

When our grief is fresh, we cannot see beyond the next hour or next decision. We have more questions than answers. We don't know how we will continue without our loved one, with our divorce, or with this illness. Our lives have forever changed and we are scared.

I found that as time went on, the anxiety lessened. I was beginning to find answers to questions like, "Should I stay in my house?" For me I decided to stay at least for now. I found a trustworthy gardener to keep the outside the way I wanted it. I couldn't maintain the inside of the house and keep the outside maintained as we always had. This, believe it or not, was a big stress for me. Yes, I had many family and friends to help out but I did not want to be dependent on them forever. I needed to find long term people to help me like a plumber, carpet cleaners and a pool service company. I knew I could not maintain my home, inside and out, by myself. Upon working out some of these details I felt my stress level go down.

What is it you need to do to make you feel less anxious? What decisions do you need to make? Ask your friends for suggestions of reputable people and services. Do what you can afford to make your life more manageable.

If it is your finances, seek a friend who may be in the financial world, or a trusted friend or family member to give you some suggestions. Hire a financial professional to look over your situation. If you are financially in a bad way, you may need to sell your house or down-size. I sold three vehicles and I was able to buy a newer car. Don't make any major decisions for a year, because your emotions and thoughts are too scattered. But as you can, make smaller decisions to help you survive this time. If you can afford it _____, do it. Even a small decision can make a world of difference.

I had always told myself that if something happened to Jim first, I would sell the house and move into an apartment. My daughter and I went to look at some rental homes and we decided they would be too confining for me at this time. I looked online at apartments and realized that staying in my house was the best decision for now. I love my home. It is a comfortable Santa Fe house which is full of memories that Jim and I made for over twenty-four years. The walls hold much laughter and I can remember the fun times and holidays we shared with family and friends.

Run your questions and concerns by trusted friends and family and let some time go by without making any major decisions. Ask for prayer from others and when confused don't do anything rash. You see, after a major loss, we are always trying to numb the pain. We think a move, a big expenditure, or 'whatever' will make us feel better. Sometimes, we do feel better for a while, but we are not really capable, at that time, to make a big decision or change. You want something....anything... to make you feel better. You really want your old life back. You want your husband you have loved for over fifty-three years back. You don't want to have to make these decisions. But eventually you will have to. If possible, take the year the experts suggest and give yourself that time. By forcing matters, I found out my anxiety level went up. I also realized I did not have the energy or stamina to take on a move or any major change. Eventually, after some months passed, I found my anxiety not as overwhelming, and things weren't so unsettled. But, without warning, I could have a day that it all came crashing down on me.

Yes, anxiety and fear do accompany the grief journey. Given your circumstances, it is inevitable. However, if you cannot function, you should go talk to a doctor, counselor, or your pastor. It is hard to know what to expect at this time and when you may need some professional help. Grief recovery groups or talking to a friend on a regular basis are helpful. I started praying with a dear, safe friend weekly.

Anxiety and fear can be dispelled through reading God's word and claiming His promises like never before. It is in times of grief and loss that we can't just 'talk the talk'; we have to stand on what we know as truth. That is why we must 'know it before we need it." God instructs us to 'fear not' and 'do not be anxious.' You say, "Sure God, that's easy for YOU to say, You are God." But, remember, everything you have ever experienced or felt, He has felt as well. Jesus experienced the death of a loved one, agony, pain and betrayal. There is nothing we will go through that God has not already gone through. NOTHING! Remember, whether we feel His presence or not, He is with us at all times and when we are too weak, He will carry us.

On a very practical note I started exercising at the gym again. I know exercise helps but it was a hard thing for me to resume because Jim and I had always done this together. There are some basic things we can do to help ourselves going through this journey.

"Fear not, for I have redeemed
you; I have summoned you by
name; you are mine."
(Isaiah 43:1)

"Consider Him who endured
such opposition from sinful men,
so that you will not grow weary
and lose heart."
(Hebrews 12:3)

"'Quietness' is the classroom
where you learn to hear
My voice."
– (Jesus Calling Oct. 30)[2]

CHAPTER 11

THE FIVE STAGES OF GRIEF

"He has sent me to bind up the brokenhearted, to proclaim freedom for the captives, and release from darkness for the prisoners, to proclaim the year of the Lord's favor....to comfort all who mourn, and provide for those who grieve in Zion... to bestow on them the oil of gladness instead of mourning."[1]

For years I have read about the five stages of grief. I am now living them. There are many authors who have listed other stages of grief but from the reliable sources of Elisabeth Kubler-Ross,[2] I am sharing the five main ingredients of grief. Mind you, you most likely will not go from one stage to another in an orderly fashion. You may jump from one to the other or have to go through a couple of stages at one time. As I've shared before, the journey of grief is unpredictable and our own journey. If you stay in one stage longer than others, don't worry, you will move on when you are ready and as your heart and emotions begin to heal. You may go back to a stage months later. There is no right or wrong way to manage grief. Deep sorrow shows itself in many ways, but these are the main five stages that most people have experienced.

So, let's go through them one by one. If your heart is broken, or you've suffered a loss, I'm sure you will recognize these various stages.

Stage 1 – **Denial.** I didn't realize for a few weeks after Jim's death that I really was in denial. How can you be in denial when you go to bed alone and wake up alone? Quietly, I kept telling myself that Jim was coming back. Maybe he's just on a trip. I believe with all my heart that God could raise him from the dead and if we prayed hard enough that just might happen. I remember going to the movies with my daughter and daughter-in-law and through the movie I was thinking, "Is Jim really gone or is he home waiting for me?" Your mind really does play tricks on you and you keep having 'reality checks' so to speak. 'Is Jim really gone?' 'Did he really die or is this all a bad dream?' And then your memories bring you back to reality. Yes, he did die.

I remember the days in the hospital by his bed with tubes all connected to him. I remember that morning we got the call to quickly come to the hospital. I can still hear the doctor say to me on the phone, "Mrs. Knipe your husband threw a blood clot this morning and we have been doing CPR for 30 minutes and you need to get here." That was the saddest phone call anyone can receive. Your loved one is dying or maybe has already died in a hospital room, in a car accident, hit by a drunk driver, or from medical complications. No matter the cause, this is not a phone call you want to ever receive.

I believe the state of denial is for our own protection in the early weeks and months of grieving. It is like a protective bubble around us until we can look at and process what really is happening. Denial keeps the hard blow from hitting us too soon. Of course, we must come to the place of reality but that is different for all of us. It may take months to get to the place of looking at our loss and making it real. This *really* is happening. I did lose my career, I did lose my spouse, I did lose my child, I did lose my marriage.

We may want to stay in denial, but in time, we will be awakened to other strong feelings and stages of grief. As denial turns into reality, we will hurt deeper and face what is really going on around us.

Denial as a real stage of grief holds its own reality of what we are feeling at that particular time. We may be denying the loss but feelings of other emotions begin to come alive.

Stage 2 – Depression. Almost one month to the day I moved from denial to depression. That adrenalin I was living with just seemed to dry up. You are thrown into the dark pit of reality. Your loved one is not coming back. Your diagnosis is not good. The fatal accident *did* happen. Your life will never be the same again. You have a huge hole in your heart that only your loved one can fill. As far as a death, we know that time heals. We know that God will heal that gaping wound, but healing takes time.

At this stage of grieving, you need to be very careful you don't step over into despair and stay there. Make sure you don't sink too deep. This is the time you call friends and family members for an extra dose of prayer. If needed go see a doctor, therapist, or grief counselor. Take inventory each day and sometimes each moment to make sure you're feeling what is normal for this stage. Please don't overmedicate unless prescribed by a doctor. Don't dwell on suicidal thoughts and don't seclude yourself from others. Be around other people even if you don't want to. There is hope and you will eventually get on the other side. Some of the lies you may believe during this stage are, "Things will never get better." "My heart will never heal." "I can't live without my loved one." "I will not be able to function again."

In my situation, having met Jim at such a young age and marrying him at age eighteen, the hole in my heart was pretty big. Over half a century I have loved this man. No it was not all bliss. We had financial troubles, years with a prodigal child, and years of recovery from being hurt in ministry. So, my depression ran deep and my biggest question was, "What will I do without him?" "How will I go on living?"

Ask yourself, "Where is my deepest pain?" "Where is my deepest hurt?" I told myself I couldn't go on without him. And at that time, I truly believed that. So, you find yourself in the mire of depression and you feel hopeless, desperate and without purpose.

The good news is that we are never hopeless and even this stage will not last forever. One day at a time, I was moving forward. I would have joy again because God promises to turn our mourning into joy.

Again, place yourself in 'survival mode' and do whatever you have to do to make it through to the next moment. Call a friend, invite yourself to someone's home, do something you enjoy like hiking, shopping, biking, or some kind of creative activity such as woodworking or scrapbooking. I find that making my own greeting cards is very therapeutic for me in my 'dark' times. It's helpful to create something during these times. It was during this time that I began to think about writing this book.

One day I was feeling exceptionally lonely and desperate. I prayed, "Please, Father, are you there? Help me!" Seriously, I heard the Lord answer me, "I'm here and I'm carrying you." Sometimes we can't walk or stand, and we need to be carried. Like the picture of the shepherd with the sheep across his shoulders, we need to be carried and comforted in a way only He knows how to do.

During your journey of grief, you find out who your safe, good friends are. Because no matter what stage you are going through, they are there. They are there to do whatever it is you need. They are willing to come sit with you, bring you dinner, pray with you over the phone, or whatever the need may be. I remember during this stage I broke my coffeepot. The thought of no coffee the next morning was more than I could handle. Even though I did not want to go out at 8:30 at night and get a new coffeepot, I knew I would really regret this in the morning. I am one of those people who have to have their coffee as soon as they wake up. So, I went out and bought a new coffeepot. Later I told my oldest son that I went and purchased a new coffeepot the night before and he said he would have gladly done that for me. That's what a true friend or family member would do! They 'come alongside' of you no matter what the need. No coffee in the AM would have been a disaster!

If you are experiencing any physical problems, such as intestinal problems, do not hesitate to see a physician. My sister lost her husband suddenly to a heart malfunction. She suffered diverticulitis requiring major surgery several months after he died. Lack of sleep or interrupted sleep patterns can add to your depression as well. Keep an eye on yourself.

Remember, you will not stay in this stage of depression either. If you do for a very long period of time, I highly suggest you seek professional help.

My prayer for you is from Numbers 6:24; "The Lord bless you and keep you; the Lord make his face shine upon you and be gracious to you, the Lord turn his face toward you and give you peace."

Stage 3 – Anger. "But I'm not an angry person", you say. By nature, you may not be given to anger, but after a major loss you may find yourself angry for a lot of reasons. You could feel anger towards God for letting your situation happen. You feel angry at your "X" because of the divorce. You may even feel angry at your loved one for leaving you. Your anger can take many forms.

One day I got up and felt so angry. I mentioned earlier that I was mad at Jim that day for leaving me with all the duties of our home and outside upkeep. He was one of those men who knew how to do most anything and he kept the outside of our home immaculate. We shared our financial responsibility together and I felt the heavy burden of all that being on my shoulders now. You may feel the heaviness of raising your children alone or having to care for yourself without your mate or whatever your loss has left for you to care for. I know I wasn't really angry at Jim. He did not choose to die on August 1st, but I felt abandoned that particular day and was angry that he had died and was not coming back. There is that reality again!

A lot of people get angry at God. I don't think I did. I questioned God for taking Jim but I knew that God knew what was best. Again, I know that our days are numbered. There is no arguing that fact, *except* if someone is the victim of a tragedy or takes their own life. I don't know how that plays into the whole picture of God's eternal plan.

It's alright to express your anger, even at God. He can take it. But don't act out that anger at those around you. Look at it and pray about it and talk with someone if you need to. In time, anger will turn into bitterness and bitterness will turn into unforgiveness and that is not good. The Bible states very clearly, "Get rid of all bitterness, rage and anger..."[3] You can't stay mad at God for months and years for if you do, your heart will become hardened. I have witnessed people who have stayed angry at God for something and they are usually people who are not pleasant to be around. God cannot work in us if we remain an angry person. However, we do need to go through the angry stage and release all that anger to God. He can forgive us as soon as we recognize what we have done and ask forgiveness. Imagine me questioning the Almighty. But God understands our pain and hurt.

While praying for Jim's healing, I boldly asked God what happened to all those prayers offered on Jim's behalf.

August 19, 2017 Journal Entry:

> "Eight days after Jim died, God answered, "I heard every one of them (the prayers) and I was pleased. I tell you in my word, to 'pray continually,'⁴ and you did. You all did. But, remember, My ways are different than your ways. In the scope of the "big picture" this was the better way for Jim. I created him and knew every day he would live on this earth, and I knew the day he would 'come home.' Trust Me in this and don't let your faith waver. I am still the God of the universe and I see the whole plan. I am the potter and you are the clay."⁴

God is bigger than our anger. He is able to handle it. Just don't stay there for an exceptionally long period of time. Work through *why* you are angry with God. Share your feelings with a safe confidant. Remember, your feelings and your emotions are yours. Don't hide them, own them. Picture Jesus standing in front of you with his arms out and He is saying to you, "Give me all your pain."

Stage 4 – Bargaining. What is there to bargain about with loss? When our situation starts to 'go south,' when our loved one is gravely ill, our marriage is in shambles, or that tragic accident happened we had no warning of, we begin to bargain with God. "But God, IF you will turn this around, I will _____." I will never be mad again. I will never holler at my kids again. I will give my life to you, if you will only give my child back to me." We bargain and we don't even realize it. It is like a 'foxhole' experience. "I will do this _____, God, if you do _____." We desperately want the situation reversed. We want our loved one back, our child alive, or our marriage back to the good old days. We never appreciate something so much as when it is taken from us.

I try to have a thankful heart every day and thank God for my family and friends, my health and His provision. I have always been grateful for my marriage, my husband, and Jim's ability to provide for our family. I am thankful for having God in my life. Do not take your life for granted. Enjoy what you have, while you have it. Circumstances can change so quickly. What is here today may be gone tomorrow with life never being the same.

We don't know how long each stage of grief will last. *Feel* what you feel each day. Bargain if you must, but more importantly change anything that God may desire for you to change as part of your healing. Maybe you need to change from complaining about everything to being more grateful. Maybe you need to stop taking things for granted and be more appreciative. Possibly you are to look outside yourself and look to the needs of others. Live outside your comfort zone by doing things you normally wouldn't choose to do.

Once the worst of the grieving journey is behind you, reevaluate your life and see if there are any changes needed for you to live a more fulfilled life for others and Christ.

Each of the stages will come and go. You may go through one stage a lot longer than another, and that's okay. Again, if months have gone by and you are unable to deal with life at all, please seek professional help. I'm not saying you will not continue to have strong waves of sorrow and sadness. After my two trips to meet my new great-grandsons, I came home so sad and missing Jim terribly. You never know what will trigger you to feel that deep sorrow again. We must deal with it in time but there's no hurry. The journey is rough and takes time and a lot of energy.

Stage 5 – Acceptance does not mean putting your grief aside. It doesn't mean you are now 'whole' again or that you are 'ok' with the situation. It does mean you have come to the place in this journey that you finally 'accept' the fact that your loss has really happened and is reality. We begin to move forward, ever so slightly and start to get involved with other people and their concerns. I found this to be most helpful, so I invited several friends to come over weekly for fellowship and prayer. This was part of God's healing for me. I was uplifted when I opened my doors and heart to others. Did I still have my very sad times? Yes! But I began to feel *'alive'* again.

I still did not have to like what happened to me, but I was accepting it as something God would use greatly in my life. 'Life' itself began to take on meaning and, most days, I got up with anticipation of the day and what God had for me. Now, acceptance may not happen this quickly for you. Your hardship may take a lot longer for you to accept. Accept this as well. As I am writing this I am listening to the song, *King of My Heart*,[5] where the words are repeated throughout the song, *"He is good...and He is never going to let me down."* Even in my darkest moments I can declare, "You are good."

So why did this happen to me? Why did this happen to you?"

I don't know, but I do know that my God will use our loss for our good and His glory if, we let Him.

Coming to the place of acceptance with your loss does not mean you will never question 'why' again. Over six months after Jim's death I found myself questioning *why* the heart doctor did not schedule Jim's surgery sooner than August. Jim had told him in January that his symptoms were worsening and he was unable to do some of the activities he had been doing up until then. At this time, I felt I needed to talk to the heart doctor and ask that big 'why.' Maybe it would put my mind at ease, or so I hoped. It is alright to ask the 'whys' and to even ask those 'in the know'. If this will make is easier to accept then it may be worth following through. I found all I wanted was some answers. Allow yourself this freedom.

I wish I could tell you that you will work quickly through the stages of grief. But, we all walk this journey at a different pace. Some grief is harder to bear than others. Allow God to take you through this process with him. Give yourself the freedom to go at your own speed and deal with all the hurt, pain and betrayal. Give yourself permission to hurt!

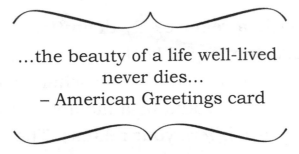

...the beauty of a life well-lived
never dies...
– American Greetings card

CHAPTER 12

"RELAPSES"

"In quietness and trust is your strength."[2]

"O Lord....be our strength every morning."[3]

What is a relapse? By definition a relapse is *'to slip or fall back into a former worse state'*.[1] *Relapses* will occur when you least expect them. It could be a memory, or a place you go that triggers your relapse. They always catch you off guard.

I remember as a young girl vacationing with my family at the Jersey Shore. My cousin and I would play in the waves and we never saw that big wave coming that knocked us to the ocean floor. You know the feeling, when you think you will drown before you come up for air. You scramble to stand upright again and you ask, "What just hit me?"

Relapses of grief are like surprise waves that hit us when we least expect them and they knock us off our feet.

It was almost six months after Jim's passing. I took a trip with my daughter, Lynn, and son-in-law, Ken, to Chico, California to meet my new great-grandson. I spent almost a week there cuddling the baby and enjoying my time with the new parents. I totally love being a great-grandmother for the third time. My grandson and his wife showed me their town of Chico and we shopped and did secondhand stores and even got to take the baby and enjoy dinner out.

The day we were flying home, I was completely caught off guard when a fresh wave of grief knocked me down. I felt waves of anxiety and sadness like in the first few weeks of losing Jim and I wanted to curl up in a ball. "What is this?" I asked myself. I realized quickly that the thoughts of returning home without Jim were too overwhelming for me. You actually think for a moment that someday you will go home and your loved one will still be there. I knew I was in my right mind, or at least I thought I was, but you do play these games at times and it's alright. You can't live in that fantasy, because the reality of the truth hits you all over again. That particular day I was not expecting this big wave.

You don't always know *what* triggers a relapse of grief. Maybe it was returning home to an empty house. Maybe it was just accepting the reality, once again, that I am alone now. When my son-in-law dropped me off at my house after several hours of travel, I felt such loneliness. It was overwhelming. I thought that maybe when I got home my life would be normal; but walking into that empty house proved that theory was wrong. You realize once again, that your life, as you knew it, had forever changed.

Remember, it takes two to three years to walk this grief journey and sometimes up to five years for a tragedy. These times of relapse are okay. For me, it had not even been six months. It was alright to feel very sad again. It was alright to feel desperate and lonely again as reality hit me like an ocean wave. Even when relapses sneak up on you and knock you flat when you least expect them, you will get up and you will survive. I turned my thoughts to that 'new' little great-grandson and the joy he brought me. Life continues, and I would be able to go on. I had so many joyful happenings around me and that became my focus.

A week later I accompanied my daughter and son-in-law to Denver to see my second 'new' great-grandson. These babies were born one week apart. In the midst of my grief there was life. Jim was like a 'baby whisperer,' he could always calm a crying baby. He had a gentle and calming way about him. He would have loved those two little babies so much.

I didn't stay in that valley long. I was very sad and missed Jim terribly, but I had so much to look forward to. Sometimes those steps forward are hard. You want to drag the past along. But you must face the duties calling you and move ahead. I still had things to take care of and bills to pay and decisions to make. So you move ahead one step at a time.

A week after returning from Chico, I attended a memorial service for a friend's mom. The chapel that the service was held in was the same chapel where we held Jim's service. Do

I go or don't I? Once again, I pulled up my big girl pants and knew it was right that I go. As I pulled open the door of the chapel, tears immediately filled my eyes. But I knew I was to be there. At times, you just have to do things even though they're hard. There are times, though, when it's alright not to attend something or go somewhere if it's too soon and too painful. Again, I had a relapse of grief, but I knew I would be alright.

It's at these times you surround yourself with safe and encouraging people. One day after I returned from one of my great-grandma trips, I invited a dear friend over for coffee. We talked, shared our hearts, and agreed to start praying together weekly. I explained my relapse with her and she comforted me. It's funny how the simple matters of a day that could consume you, help you to overcome the grief. Sitting with a friend over coffee made that day more pleasant. You have to force yourself to see *today*. Today holds many blessings, new beginnings and fresh encouragement. You may still be living in 'survival mode' and that is perfectly fine. Do what you have to do to survive that day. The mundane matters may feel overwhelming but you must force yourself to take care of them and somehow, that moves you forward. I can remember when tax time came around that first year. I felt paralyzed as I knew nothing about doing yearly taxes. After I fretted awhile, I asked for help from my tax man and my daughter-in-law and I was able to get through the process. Ask for help when needed.

Don't fight the relapses. When they strike, lean into them. Let them have their way. Feel what you feel at that time and know you will get up from this wave. It is all a part of the grief journey. Don't be discouraged that you stepped back a few steps, that is normal. Your heart is still broken and the pain of your loss is still there. Remember, the journey is one step at a time.

Be prepared for relapses to hit you on all the 'firsts.' The first holidays, anniversaries, and birthdays will be hard for you. Expect them to be hard and plan ahead, this will make it easier for you. My oldest daughter was especially good at looking ahead and planning something with me to help me survive the 'firsts.' I remember the first Valentine's Day without Jim. He would always remember that day with a small gift of flowers or candy or a lunch date. I found myself dreading the first Valentine's Day without Jim. My daughter called me several days before and invited me to dinner that evening. She also asked what my expectations were for my birthday which was in March. In her subtle way she was making sure those holidays were covered for me. I can remember hearing from so many loved ones and friends that first Valentine's Day without Jim. You will never know, unless you are grieving, how much a call, a text, or an invite helps you survive those 'firsts.'

This is a very practical way you can help your family member or friend get through those very hard days. Put it on your calendar to contact them. It will mean everything to them.

One step at a time
One breath at a time
One word at a time
One day at a time
Be gentle with yourself
Give yourself time
(A text from Donna Edwards)

CHAPTER 13

YOUR LEGACY "WHAT ARE 'YOU' LEAVING BEHIND?"

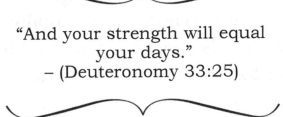

"And your strength will equal
your days."
– (Deuteronomy 33:25)

Jim's Journal Entry 2017:

"One of the simplest rules of life: act
justly, love mercy and walk humbly
with your God."[1]

I ask you, "What kind of footprints will you
leave behind?"

The Bible has several references concerning
passing our faith from one generation to the
next. We're to tell our stories of what God has
done for us to our children, grandchildren and

great- grandchildren. As of now I have three great-grandchildren. They need to hear how the faithfulness of God has been there in our married life and through our many trials. If we don't tell the next generation, who will? If we don't pray for the generations coming up, who will?

This chapter mostly deals with a person who has passed away. But since we don't know the number of our own days, it is really a lesson for all of us. It is never too soon to think about 'what am I leaving behind?' 'What will people remember me for?'

A legacy means, *'something left to a person; something that has come from an ancestor or predecessor or the past.'* In the Bible we see the word *'inheritance'* and that is not always referring to a monetary gift.

Our youngest daughter was struggling with some things in her life and we were having a serious mother/daughter talk. I was reminiscing about her dad and the rich legacy he left behind. He was very intentional with what he did the last few years of his life. As we were talking about this, I looked at her and asked, "What do you want others to remember about you?" We all should ask that question from time to time, "What am I going to leave as my legacy?" "Have I _____ (fill in your own name) left my world of influence a better place?" "Has my life made a difference?" "If not, what should I begin to do to change that?"

Since each day is a gift from our Creator, how should we use that gift? First, we must open our gifts every day, see what's inside the package, and use them to the fullest. Maybe my gift today is encouragement and I am to give it to someone I meet as I go throughout my day. Perhaps my gift is an act of service which I am to gladly deliver to someone else. Maybe all I can handle today is a note to someone hurting or a text letting them know I care. There are always young men and women out there who need mentoring and encouragement as they raise children, deal with marriage, or take care of an elderly parent. A simple act of love can make someone's day. The blessing always comes back to us possibly wrapped a little different. God's word states, "Give and it shall be given to you."[2] This is such a true principle to follow.

As you consider the legacy you will leave, let's start with a few suggestions:

1. **Is there anything at all I need to set straight with my children?** After my children had all grown and left home, I wrote them a letter of apology for anything I did as a mother that hurt them, or any area of need I didn't meet. I did not want them entering adulthood or parenting with any 'baggage' I had caused, no matter how I saw it or they perceived it. I just wanted to clear the air.

2. **Is there anyone you need to forgive?** Your spouse, children, parents, family member, friend or the church in general? Forgiveness is necessary for a healthy Christin walk.

3. **Have you shared your love for Christ with future generations?** Do those around you see Christ in you? As a parent, grandparent, great-grandparent, neighbor, friend, or mentor, has your life represented your commitment to Christ?

Do your actions and words match up with your commitment?

4. **If your life ended tomorrow, are you sure you know where you will live *eternally?*** Have you made that commitment to receive Christ and eternal salvation? If not, I highly suggest you do this, as life is very fragile and can be taken at any time.

5. **Does your spouse know how much you love and appreciate him (her)**? Have you thanked them lately for what they have added to your life? Have they been a good provider for you? A good spiritual leader? Has your spouse been kind to you and let you be 'who' you are? Have they been a good spiritual leader in your home? Have they made wise decisions with your finances, business, and family? I am not saying everyone has had a great family life and marriage, but with God's help, we can improve and change in the areas needed. We have to want to change though and surrender our life totally to Him. We will all answer to the Almighty. There will

be that day when we are standing alone before Him and he asks, "What have you done for me?" "How did you show me to others?" "Did others know Me because of you?" "Did you use your gifts and talents well that I gave you?"

I know that Jim heard the words clearly proclaimed over him when he faced his Maker, "Well done, son, well done. You have been faithful in what I gave you to manage. You have faithfully served Me and loved your wife, family and friends well. I welcome you to Heaven with open arms."

Jim left a legacy without measure. His time spent with others from family members to acquaintances made a difference. Marriages were improved because he spent time with the husbands who wanted to make their relationship better. Friends were comforted who had lost a spouse and needed to talk. He taught men's classes and we led an Adult Sunday School class for almost twenty years. He invested in youth groups and spent time with those in the hospital. He taught his kids what it meant to be a follower of Christ, to be moral and to become a responsible young man or woman. He taught our daughters and grand-daughters what it felt like to be spoiled by a man. Jim spoiled me as well. I think that's why his death has been so hard on me.

Jim attended a men's breakfast where he purposely went a little late so he could go around the table and personally hug every man there. He kept a diary of what the Lord meant to him and he always wanted to become a better man and a better Christian. He would always say to me, "I just don't feel like I'm doing enough." And I would quickly answer that he saved the lives of at least two of our children and he serves the Lord every day in quiet ways. The last few years of his life, I watched him become bolder in his faith. I saw him take the first step to reach out to someone hurting or ill. Jim never stopped growing spiritually and we found this statement in his journal written only a few weeks before he died, "I want to see Jesus this year like never before." And...he did. He saw Jesus face to face on August 1, 2017.

While visiting one of my grandsons, he told me he started a men's breakfast in his area that met monthly, just like Papa. What a memorial.

What will your legacy be? It is never too late to change the direction of your life, to get help for your addiction, to make the Lord first priority, to start attending a church, or make better choices. Remember, God will meet you exactly where you are. He is just waiting for you to respond to his call. He yearns for you to come to him and he loves you in spite of your choices, in spite of your past, and the road you may be walking at this moment.

God is a God of *second chances*. He is a God who restores, redeems, forgives, and He forgets everything we confess. Our Abba Father wipes us off and sets us on solid ground. He will take our hand and guide us. He has been waiting with outstretched arms.

He will gently carry us when we are too broken. How can you refuse a God like that?

Jim knew his God and had no doubts where he would spend eternity. He lived a life worthy of God's approval and he finished well. Will you do the same? We all leave some kind of legacy behind. Is your legacy one that is life-giving? Are you finishing the course set out for you? Remember, you were created with a purpose. It is our responsibility to fulfill the destiny we were called to.

September 5, 2017 Journal Entry:

> "And so I have decided that my only choice is to move forward, pain and all, and see what the Father has for me. As Ephesians 5 instructed me, 'to live as children of light....not darkness...and find out what pleases the Lord. Have nothing to do with the fruitless deeds of darkness and be careful how you live. Be filled with the Spirit and always give thanks to God for everything.' This...is the way, walk in it."

God had spelled out His plan for me. There is life after sorrow and I am to make the most of every opportunity and understand what the Lord's will is for me.

2017 Jim's Journal Entry:

> "Key to life and death – Do Colossians
> 3 every day, all the time. Get this
> right and we will be most like Jesus
> as we can possibly be of this side of
> glory; which is why God created us
> in the first place."

One of Jim's biggest legacies was his prayers for others. Many nights he was awakened at 3:00 a.m. and would pray for friends and family and those in need. We have a neighbor that was quite ill with no diagnosis. The doctors could not figure out what was going on with him. In the middle of the night Jim would have his prayer vigil. After several weeks of Jim's diligent praying, we saw our neighbor and he said the doctor had come up with a diagnosis of a rare disease. Once they diagnosed him, they began the proper treatment and our friend began to improve. Jim's prayers made a difference. He took his calling of an intercessor seriously and never minded being awakened at night to fulfill what he had been called to do. Jim was intentional and he was a servant.

He never wanted the recognition. Jim's journal said it all. He even wrote a praise song that my daughter stills sing to this day.

Shortly after her Dad's death, our youngest daughter told me the thing she missed the most about her Dad, was that he was her *coach*. He would listen well and encourage her along the way.

Leaving a legacy does not mean you have to be important by today's standards. It does not mean you have to accumulate a lot of money and possessions to hand down. But it does mean you live your life worthy of God's calling and you accomplish those things He has called you to fulfill. It is a life well lived. At Jim's memorial service the pastor said this, "Jim will be dearly missed, but always treasured. Memories are our most treasured possessions that cannot be lost or stolen. Two things Jim wanted for all of us is to: 1. Come to a relationship with God through turning to Jesus. 2. To seize every day you're given. Jim encouraged us to celebrate others, champion people, love better, and love bolder each passing day."

"Acknowledge and take to heart this day that the Lord is God in heaven above and on the earth below. There is no other. Keep his decrees and commands....so that it may go well with you and your children after you and that you may live in the land the Lord your God gives you for all time."[4]

Ask yourself every day, "Will my decisions and choices today, make a difference in someone else's life for the better?"
– Sally J. Knipe

CHAPTER 14

WHAT'S NEXT?

"See to it that you complete
the work you have received
in the Lord."[1]

What do I do now? Some of the heavy trauma of grief is behind me and I feel I can look ahead. Not too far though. But can I see my future? No. Like all of us, I do not know what my future holds. I just know that I have an emptiness in my heart that will be there a long, long time. My loss has made me a different person. I hope a better person. All suffering leaves a mark on us. I pray a better mark. I pray I am more compassionate toward others and not a bitter person because of my loss. I hope I love deeper, and that I am not afraid to take chances in loving others. I pray I have a deeper sense of who God is, and how much He desires to take care of me, heal me, and give me newness of life.

I know I'm not done. As long as I have breath, I have purpose. As long as I can speak, I can pray. As long as I can think, I can make a difference in someone else's life, every single day. I can still hug, encourage, build up, show appreciation, be grateful and live each day to its fullest. Yes, my heart still hurts, but even in my pain, I can bless those around me. You see, it's *not* about me, it's all about Him. Even in my grief journey, it's about Him leading me, healing me, loving me and restoring my soul so I can serve Him better.

Yes, I still cry in bed alone at night. I still want Jim back. I still desire things to be as they were. But I still have a life even though I have loss. My heart will heal eventually, but not without scars. All suffering leaves scars, but scars are good if we learn from them and grow more Christ-like. I know Romans 8:28a that says, "All things work together for good..." can be controversial to some. You may say, "How is losing my child good?" "How is losing my marriage good?" "How is watching my husband suffer good?" We may not be at the place of accepting our loss as *good*, but we can know that God is not done yet with whatever He is doing through our grief.

Whatever your loss and tragedy is, your heart will heal. Life will get better and the pain will eventually subside, because we serve a loving God whose purpose is to renew and restore us. We will look different because we *are* different. Jesus grows us through pain and trials like no other way.

God still has a very important purpose for your life after grief. My pain has not been wasted and neither has yours. For God wastes nothing in our lives. We will feel joy again, we will dance again, and we will serve with more purpose.

If you had asked me nine months ago what I would do if Jim passed away, I would have said I would crawl up in a ball and go to bed the rest of my life. I wanted to right after he died and everyone had left after the memorial service. I remember the day I had the choice to crawl back in bed, or do something a little constructive. I chose to put my house back together and go forward. What a hard, hard choice that was. Each day since then, I have had that choice to go forward or stay stuck in the awful pain of grief.

No one ever said this 'grief journey' is easy. It is hard and rugged and goes on and on. But most days, I see a rainbow. I feel loved by others and especially by my Father. I find His mercies new every morning. Like beautiful gifts to open each day. This morning as I got up and looked outside, the clouds were a beautiful, puffy piece of art over the mountains.

I will make it through but not without struggle. I can live with purpose even with a hurting heart. Even though I live with pain, I can look forward to the future. Some days it takes everything in me to get up and find purpose. Grief has no limit and no timeline. It is an individual journey we each walk. But, I have good memories and I wish the same for you. Remember the 'good' things of your relationship with the person you lost. Dwell, with hope, that a day will come when you will find joy again in living. Do not stay in the quicksand of bad memories and unforgiveness.

Jim and I didn't have one of those 'let's just get through this' marriage. When you marry the 'right' person, and they pass away, there are no regrets. That is one less thing you have to grieve.

As your grief begins to subside, pick your activities carefully. Don't throw yourself into 'busyness' just to dull the pain. You must walk the entire journey to be healthy. Busyness can be a deterrent, but it doesn't help you heal. Sometimes, it just puts it off. You must work through your grief. I really took my time getting back involved with former commitments. And if I became involved too soon, I stepped back. You think activities are good to fill your time, but they can be detrimental, if you are not ready.

In some situations, like divorce, you have to work and be responsible for your children and everything else you were left with. This can be overwhelming. Only do those things you have to do until you get through the worst of your grief. Ask for help and try to slow your life down as best as you can. You must grieve your loss, but take time for you. Parenting alone takes so much energy, and it can be devastating to add a major loss to your life.

But life does go on. Eventually it will be like waking up from a long sleep. You will feel again and laugh again and find joy. You will serve again and find new meaning to your life. You will heal and that darkness of grief will begin to subside.

As long as I live, I have purpose. I am needed and will fulfill whatever God has for me. It may be something completely new. I'm certainly not there yet, but I can be there for others and bring them hope even in my sorrow.

God wants to give us hope, hope for our future and hope as we walk through our grief journey to the end. We will never stop loving our loved one that we loss, but we must go forward. We will come out of the valley and stand on the mountain again. Yes, you will still experience those 'dark days' as I call them. Even after six months I would wake up and not want to live another day without Jim. I found that just telling a close friend or family member how I was feeling that day really took the sting out of it. You have to release your pain.

Even though you are not through the valley, I pray this book has helped you in some way. I pray your dark days get fewer, that you have hope in Jesus, and experience His peace in the midst of your journey through grief. I pray you feel the closeness of your Heavenly Father's presence. You are not alone. Your pain will lessen and you will find a purpose-filled life again. For God will turn your mourning into joy. Blessings to you.......

"I am so sorry for your loss of
someone special or of something.
I do know in time, God will make
something good out of your
tragedy. Don't look for it now,
just look at the moment in front
of you and God will give you what
you need for that moment. His
beautiful piece of workmanship
is not complete, and there are
still many strokes of the brush to
come, but we will be a beautiful
piece in His art gallery when
He is finished.""
– Sally J. Knipe

"Even though we are missing that special someone or something.... and even though we are forever changed, we will become whole again but in a different way."
– Sally J. Knipe

"The death of a beloved is an amputation." By C.S. Lewis

"Part of us will always be missing. We may feel like we can't go on, but we do and we will become whole even though that part of us is gone." – Sally J. Knipe

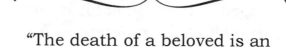

THE JOURNEY OF GRIEF

by Sally J. Knipe

You heard my cry.
My spirit's weak.
I've lost my way.
I have no peace.

My life is empty.
My loved one gone.
Where is my joy?
Where is my song?

I feel so alone.
The valley is deep.
The darkness is heavy.
I can only weep.

"Look up, look up,
I've seen your tears.
I've heard your cry.
I know your fears."

"I've walked your journey,
I know your grief,
It's at this time,
You must believe."

"Your faith is strong,
I'll show the way.
You know my Word,
I've heard you pray."

"When you are weak,
And the journey's long,
I will carry you through,
I will give you my song."

"So shed your garments,
Your garments of grief.
I'll take your pain
Your sorrow's brief."

"For I will carry you,
My love abounds.
And I will set you,
Upon solid ground."

"So, shed those grave clothes,
A new person you'll be.
Watch me work,
I'll set you free."

"Free to serve me,
Free to be,
That very person,
You're meant to be."

"With scars of sorrow,
And tears that stain
I will make you new,
You **will** live again."

"I will breathe fresh air,
Into your spirit
You will fly like an eagle,
You will love much deeper."

"So, shed those garments,
That weigh you down.
For I will set you
Upon solid ground."

"I've carried you through,
As a shepherd with his sheep.
No more will you live,
In the valley of grief."

EPILOGUE

My journey is far from over. However, I have made it this far. We can only look at one day, sometimes one hour at a time. I don't know where you are in your journey of grief, but I know you will make it through. Why? Because God says we will by taking His hand and letting Him lead us. We have no other rock to lean on.

About seven months into my journey a dear Christian brother told me that my foundation was not totally in Christ. I need to go further down. My foundation was still on some sand which does not hold us firm. I felt like the 'waves' of life were still knocking me off my feet. Our feet must be firmly planted on rock, not sand. So, I encourage you to 'go down' deeper with your faith and put your trust in him a hundred percent. That is the only thing that will hold us through this time of healing and restoration.

Don't let anyone tell you to hurry through your grief. You take as long as you need to heal. May God bless each of you as you walk this difficult journey.

Sally J. Knipe

ENDNOTES

Chapter 2–Go into 'Survival Mode'
1. *New International Version Bible*/ Tyndale House Publishers, Inc.1 Peter 5:10.

Chapter 4 – Grieve Your Own Way
1. NIV Matthew 5:4.

Chapter 6 – Where is YOUR Faith?
1. *The Hiding Place* by Corrie Ten Boon.
2. *The Message Bible* by Eugene H. Peterson, Philippians 4:19

Chapter 7 – The Whys and What Ifs
1. NIV Lamentations 3: 2.
2. NIV Romans 8:28.
3. English Standard Version Bible published in 2001 by Crossway, Psalm 139:16.

Chapter 9 – 'The Widow's Mite'

1. NIV Isaiah 46:4.
2. NIV Exodus 22:22-23.
3. NIV Psalm 68: 5-6.
4. NIV James 1:27.
5. NIV Isaiah 54:5.

Chapter 10 – Anxiety and Fear

4. NIV 1 Peter 5:7
5. *Jesus Calling* by Sarah Young, Thomas Nelson, Inc.

Chapter 11 – The Five Stages of Grief

1. NIV Isaiah 61:1-3.
2. Titles of the Five Stages of Grief from *On Death and Dying* by Elisabeth Kubler-Ross.
3. NIV Ephesians 4:31.
4. NIV 1 Thessalonians 4:17.
5. *King of My Heart* CD by Bethel Music.

Chapter 12–Relapses

1. *Merriam-Webster Dictionary* (American English).
2. NIV Isaiah 30:15.
3. NIV Isaiah 33:2.

Chapter 13 – Your Legacy – What are YOU Leaving Behind?

1. NIV Micah 6:8.
2. NIV Luke 6:38.
3. NIV Deuteronomy 33:25.
4. NIV Deuteronomy 4:39-40.

Chapter 14 – What's Next?

1. NIV Colossians 4:14.

OTHER RESOURCES

1. "How to Settle a Loved One's Affairs"
   digitalcommunications@azasrs.gov

2. "Being Prepared" Booklet
   HR.AZ.GOV/PDF/BEING_PREPARED_
   BOOKLET.PDF

3. "When God is Silent" by Charles R. Swindoll

4. "Life after Loss" by Bob Deits, M.Th.